# CARITAS

# CARITAS

*Tintoretto and the Scuola Grande di San Rocco, Venice*

## Brian Leslie Bishop

### FOREWORD BY
## Franco Posocco

RESOURCE *Publications* · Eugene, Oregon

CARITAS
Tintoretto and the Scuola Grande di San Rocco, Venice

Resource Publications
An Imprint of Wipf and Stock Publishers
199 W. 8th Ave., Suite 3
Eugene, OR 97401

www.wipfandstock.com

PAPERBACK ISBN: 978-1-7252-8747-1
HARDCOVER ISBN: 978-1-7252-8748-8
EBOOK ISBN: 978-1-7252-8750-1

Manufactured in the U.S.A.                                    11/12/20

For Jenny who took me there in the first place.

For Alice, Fynn, and Cai whom,
I trust, will take themselves there.

Inasmuch as ye did it not to one of the least of these,
ye did it not to me.[1]

. . . I have ta'en / Too little care of this . . . [2]

1. Matt 25:45 (KJV).
2. Shakespeare, *King Lear,* 3.4.37–38.

# CONTENTS

# ILLUSTRATIONS

Fig. 20. Jacopo Robusti called Tintoretto. *The Crucifixion* (1565) with gratitude for the generosity of the *Scuola Grande di San Rocco.* | 64

Fig. 21 Jacopo Robusti called Tintoretto. *The Crucifixion* (detail). PD Wikimedia Commons. | 75

# FOREWORD

The fifth centenary of the birth of Jacopo Tintoretto, celebrated in 2018/19, has aroused vast interest all over the world, through the organization of exhibitions, the publication of research and other manifestations of attention towards the work of the great artist.

The appeal of his message, however, does not seem to have diminished in the current year, despite the difficulties caused by the Covid-19 epidemic, if we consider that new initiatives are being launched to better understand the paintings of the Venetian painter. This is the case of the publication of Brian Bishop, an English author, who seems to continue a tradition of love for Venice and its civilization that began at least with John Ruskin, but perhaps earlier. In his careful reading of the images in sequence, he focuses above all on the contents of a religious nature and at the same time on the socio-cultural conditions of the city in the second half of the sixteenth century, when, between wars, plagues and political upheavals, there is also the great comparison between the Lutheran Reformation and the Roman Catholic Counter-Reformation.

Venice with its freedoms and mercantilism seems to want to safeguard religious tolerance and artistic autonomy when these conditions are questioned elsewhere. Brian Bishop's analysis therefore focuses on the main works of Jacopo Tintoretto, both in dogmatic and symbolic terms, as well as anthropological, content and formal, in order to arouse a discussion, which today appears very important for the understanding of that troubled period of the history of Europe and the evolution of western painting. A compelling and stimulating book, moreover well documented and offering several new insights. Moving from one picture to another in the various rooms of the Scuola Grande di San Rocco, Brian Bishop describes the painter's narration, composition and message, taking into account the cultural context, the dialogue with contemporaries, especially Titian and Veronese, as well as the contradictions and ongoing debates in the city and elsewhere.

A book interesting for the interpretation and the problems it poses, and important for the contribution to the current discussion and deepening understanding of the work of a central painter in the development of Venetian and Italian art between the Renaissance and Baroque.

A big thank you from the Scuola Grande to the author.

Franco Posocco
Guardian Grando of the Scuola Grande di San Rocco

# PREFACE

I love Venice. Therefore, I love Tintoretto. Therefore, I love the *Scuola Grande di San Rocco*. I have been visiting all three for many years and was planning to do so again this year, 2020. However, along with everyone else, I have been told to stay at home due to the pandemic. So I thought that I would do a virtual tour of the *Scuola* to which Tintoretto dedicated a lifetime's work. The purpose was to record my personal responses to the paintings and to put these responses into some sort of coherent order. The result printed in this booklet is offered as one person's informal guide to encourage readers to visit this amazing collection of a lifetime's work in one accessible location. The work of one of the world's greatest artists in one of the world's most beautiful and amazing cities. VENICE.

As a further incentive, the collection culminates in what many regard as the world's greatest ever work of art, Tintoretto's *Crucifixion*.

Please visit the *Scuola Grande di San Rocco* if at all possible.

*I am Brian Bishop an eighty-one year old retired teacher of English and World Literature. On retirement in 2005 I gained a master's degree in theology. My dissertation was on the theology of the passion frescoes of Giotto in the Scrovegni Chapel, Padua. Since then I have had two books published by Wipf and Stock in America:*

*"The Continuing Dialogue: an Investigation into the Artistic Afterlife of the Five Narratives Peculiar to the Fourth Gospel."*

*"The Beauty of Holiness. Giotto's Passion Frescoes as a Prelude to the Artistic Afterlife of The Supper at Emmaus."*

# ACKNOWLEDGEMENTS

I would like to thank the Guardian Grando, the Secretariate, and all the support staff for their understanding help and advice. Especially, I thank them for the magnificent high resolution images and the permission to publish them so readily granted.

# INTRODUCTION

## Tintoretto's Venice

The Protestant Reformation[1] in northern Europe had reper-
cussions in the South and particularly in "God's Chosen
City," Venice. Tintoretto was born in Venice in 1519, two years
after Luther's dramatic public protest in Wittenberg. From 1522
to about 1648 a period of Catholic Reform was taking place in
response to events in northern Europe. The Council of Trent met
over an eighteen-year period[2] and the Catholic Church became
more dedicated to the work of evangelization. Institutional structures such as the Society of Jesus were established and existing
structures such as the Carmelites were strengthened. Doctrine
and piety were energized. The religious mysticism associated with
this renewal movement was vigorously promoted in Venice. Traditionally, Venice has been regarded as somewhat isolated or even
immune from the effects of the Catholic reforming zeal, tolerant of
divergent religious views, and stubbornly anti-papal. Certainly, it
was a tolerant state dominated by a merchant capitalist elite where
foreign merchants operated freely. The concept of "God's Chosen
City" was based upon the mythology surrounding the transference
of Saint Mark's body to Venice from Alexandria. This event is to
be seen depicted in a mosaic above the southern transept of St.
Mark's Basilica. Venice now had apostolic patronage that placed

1. Usually dated from 1517.
2. 1545 to 1563.

1

her on a spiritual level only rivaled by Rome. Doge Giustiniano Participzio ordered a chapel built in his garden to receive the Saint and thus St. Marks—the Ducal Chapel—took precedence over San Pietro di Castello which until 1807 was the cities official patriarchal Cathedral. The Cathedral became overshadowed by St. Marks that was associated from the outset with the civil rather than the religious authorities. Whilst the view that Venice was historically independent and anti-papal, may be substantiated if one focuses on the politics of the Republic, within the many lay confraternities a closer interest in central Catholic doctrinal developments might be seen. In the Republic of Venice, spiritual and charitable associations were referred to as *scuole* that literally translates as schools. In the rest of Italy the name for a comparable institution was a *confraternita* or a brotherhood. One of the most important tasks of such an association was the spiritual care of the dying and their burial, as well as general care for the poor.

There were a large number of local *Scuole piccoli* (small) and a few influential and wealthy *Scuole grandi*. *The Scuola Grande di San Rocco* dedicated to the plague-saint[3] had been formed in 1478 and was committed to charitable works on behalf of the poor and sick and it has survived to the present time. In 1564 it had moved to its current impressive premises. It is a large meetinghouse for the lay brothers of the *Scuola*. There was much local criticism at the time based upon the perception that the Scuole had lost sight of the humility upon the basis of which they had been formed. The poet Alessandro Caravia was particularly scathing. He was a neighbor of Tintoretto in *sestiere Cannaregio* and a member of *the poligrafi*.[4]

---

3. Saint Roch was invoked during various medieval plagues and because of the miracles attributed to his intercession he is labelled a patron against plagues.

4. Traditionally, the term referred to a few versatile sixteenth-century intellectuals who were willing and able to write on any subject, hence the name: they were literary "hacks." It was applied to writers and publishers but expanded to describe a reformist network amongst the artisan community in Cannaregio. Printing became an explosive industry in sixteenth-century Venice undisturbed as it was by the wars of mainland Italy. It was three times less expensive to print in Venice than it was in Rome.

Decisions based on wealth and social standing had developed and fragmented the various fraternities. The social problems caused by plague and food shortages in the earlier decades of the sixteenth century together with the Catholic Renewal offensive mounted as a response to the rise of Protestantism gave these criticisms a spiritual dimension.

Tintoretto's marriage to Faustina Episcopi with whom he had eight children sheds light upon the structure of Venetian society in the sixteenth century. Although not of the nobility, Faustina's family were high-ranking and members of the *cittadini originarii*.[5] These were those who could demonstrate three generations of Venetian descent and non-participation in artisan activity. To them alone positions in the Ducal Chancery were available and the self-interest of the *cittandini* confirmed them as staunch supporters of the oligarchic system rather than a potentially subversive element. Tintoretto's own social background is obscure. His father, Giovanni Battista Robusti, was a silk cloth dyer but whether or not he was financially involved in the production process or what his social standing was is unknown. Carlo Ridolfi was a painter and a biographer of artists. He displayed a bias towards Venetian art counterbalancing Vasari's bias towards Florentine art. Ridolfi wrote *La vita di Giacopo Robusti*[6] in 1642. This contains anecdotal evidence of Tintoretto's personality and approach to life. The famous story illustrative of a certain class tension between Jacopo and Faustina regarding the Venetian toga that her status made available to him is amusing if of doubtful authenticity. Such stories, even if invented, tend to attach to a personality of which they seem illustrative. To that extent, at least, they have some value. We are encouraged to imagine Jacopo sulkily walking along the *Fondamenta dei Mori* in his toga as Faustina watches proudly from her window only for him to take it off and drag it through the mud on turning the corner. Whatever the truth of this story or Sartre's presentation of him as a sort of class warrior, the fact that he embraced his nickname

5. Original citizens.
6. The Biography of Tintoretto.

and the diminutive form of it—Tintoretto[7]—that appears on his contract with his local church, *Madonna dell' Orto*, suggests that he felt a closer affinity with the humble than with the socially elevated. This point is strengthened by the example of his rival for commissions in Venice, Veronese, who adopted the surname of a notable aristocratic family of Verona, *Caliari*.

Tintoretto was always a controversial painter. This often appears to have been based upon the man as much as upon the work. Tintoretto did not court popularity. The attempt to elevate criticism of Tintoretto often focused upon his speed of execution. The suggestion was that he "churned out" work at great speed for financial rather than artistic reasons. Nichol's observation regarding the identification of and objection to Tintoretto's *prestezza*[8] is useful.

> Such a recognition need not mean that economic contingency cancelled out the possibility of creative volition or commitment, as certain less sympathetic contemporaries assumed.[9]

Maybe the spiritual discernment of which Paul speaks in "Corinthians"[10] is what Tintoretto seeks and what we as viewers need to bring to his paintings. Certainly, the context might suggest that to be the case. Traditionally, the Baroque Period[11] has been regarded as the time when the dramatic and emotionally affective art called for by the Council of Trent flourished under the patronage of the Jesuit Order. However, Loyola and his followers founded the Society of Jesus in 1539. It was approved by Pope Paul the third in 1540 and Loyola's spiritual exercises were also approved in 1548. This new spirituality was clearly developing before the so-called Baroque Period. It is to be observed in the period equally vaguely called Mannerist. Protestantism looked at the seven sacraments of

---

7. Little dyer.

8. A painting technique which uses a series of fast brushstrokes to create the impression of faces and objects, rather than working out their details.

9. Nichols, "Tintoretto, *prestezza* and the *poligrafi*," 77.

10. 1 Cor 2:14–16.

11. 1600–1675.

the Catholic church: Baptism, Confirmation, the Eucharist, Penance, Anointing the sick, Holy Orders, and Matrimony. It decided that only two were sacraments with gospel authority: the Eucharist and Baptism. These two needed redefining to ensure that no special powers could be claimed by church officials. The power of the word rather than visual forms was to be promoted. No higher sanctity was to be claimed by one human being over another: "We are all consecrated priests through baptism."[12] The particular sacrament that offended protestant sensibilities was the Catholic Eucharist involving the doctrine of transubstantiation. Here the priest appears to be claiming miraculous powers. Penance, similarly, gave offense as the claim here seemed to be that the priest was a channel of divine forgiveness. There could be no individual involvement in salvation: good works or charity were insignificant if regarded as a bargain with God. The sacraments were secularized and brought down to the mundane world of physical actions and material objects. These "anathemas" were aggressively countered by the Council of Trent; particularly this was so with regard to eucharistic piety. This had long been a focal point of Catholic piety; it now became the subject of particular devotion with chapels and churches as well as works of art dedicated to the Blessed Sacrament. Similarly, Mary, reduced to the level of an ordinary mother with no intercessionary power by protestant theology was identified as the symbol of the true Catholic faith with renewed energy post-Trent.

Tintoretto does seem to have been without the digressive business drive of the looming presence of Titian. Nichol's opening sentence to his 1999 study of Tintoretto is worth quoting at this point.

> Jacopo Tintoretto was born and died in Venice. He is recorded away from his native city on only a single occasion (in September 1580, when he was briefly in Mantua) and the vast majority of his work was commissioned by Venetian patrons to adorn Venetian public buildings.[13]

12. Luther, *Weimar Ausgabe*, 6: 407, 22–23.
13. Nichols, *Tradition and Identity*, 13.

Eloquent in its simplicity, this straightforward statement of fact seems to be of huge significance. This was not the way to "get on" in the Italian or European art world of the time. One has to assume that Tintoretto was not interested in getting on as the expression is usually understood. Titian clearly was. The spirituality of Tintoretto's last signed work—*The Entombment of Christ* for "San Giorgio Maggiore" cannot be missed.

Fig. 01. Jacopo Robusti called Tintoretto. *The Entombment of Christ* (1592–94) with gratitude to the Benedictine community of the Abbey of San Giorgio Maggiore, Venice for their generosity in allowing me to use this image.

The reciprocal positions of the swooning Virgin and the Crucified Christ reinforces the doctrine of the Redemptive Partnership in line with tridentine developments. Alphonsus Samerón was an influential figure at the Council of Trent. His influence on christian thinking within Venice is demonstrable. His writings show him to have been, in particular, a leading advocate for the consideration of Mary as co-redemptrix:

> Truly, Mary, very near and uniquely joined to Him, is called full of grace . . . how much He prepared that she as mother would pour out the fullest graces among us all as her sons as one who had been assumed by Christ, not of necessity, or out of weakness, but on account of the necessity to share and make clear, certainly, the goodness and glory in the mother that she should be (if it is permitted thus to speak) co-redemptrix, co-operatrix of the salvation of mankind and to whom as an individual advocate, all the faithful ought to approach and fly for help.[14]

He refers to the Mother's "co-suffering; co-misery; co-sorrowing" and suggests that she was "co-crucified."[15] These ideas are very clearly to be seen in Tintoretto's work and suggest that the preaching of such a prominent tridentine exegete was an influence on the painter and, later, on the painters of the Baroque.

In fifteenth-century Venice there were more than two hundred *Scuole*.[16] They played a crucial role against poverty and other forms of distress. They were financed by a members' tax and bequests. Each *scuola* had a patron saint and a statute to which they were committed. There were six *Scuole Grandi*, large confraternities. The rest were *Scuole Piccole*, small confraternities. These smaller organizations tended to be based within local parishes and they theologically focused on one aspect such as the eucharistic sacraments or the rosary. Sometimes they were foreign groupings strengthening the national or religious identity of their members.

14. Miravalle, *With Jesus*, 106–7.

15. Miravalle, *With Jesus*, 109.

16. The word *scuole* is the plural form of *scuola*.

Tintoretto painted a version of *Christ Washing the Disciples' Feet*, for the *Scuola del Sacramento* of *San Marcuolo* parish. This is one of a pair of exaggeratedly horizontal compositions—*laterale*—designed for the deep lateral walls of the altar of *San Marcuolo*. Such painting commissions were less prestigious than those for large altarpieces. The *Scuole del Sacramento* were confraternities dedicated to the care of the Reserved Sacrament.[17] As they were parish based, these confraternities were smaller and more egalitarian in composition and far less wealthy than the *Scuole Grande*. With their specific dedication to the Reserved Sacrament they promoted the Counter Reformation value placed upon the doctrine of Transubstantiation that had been undermined by the Reformation. *The Last Supper*, the companion painting to *Christ Washing the Disciples' Feet*, remains in the church. *Christ Washing the Disciples' Feet* was removed in 1648 and has been replaced by a copy painted by Carlo Ridolfi. The destination of the original painting is a matter of some dispute. There is one version in Museo del Prado, Madrid and another in The Shipley Art Gallery, UK. Both versions have scholarly support for their authenticity.

17. In many Christian churches some portion of the consecrated elements (the bread and the wine) is set aside and retained after the Eucharist. The reasons for this vary by traditions. Here, the reason is the belief that the bread and the wine have been transubstantiated and become the body and blood of Christ in substance.

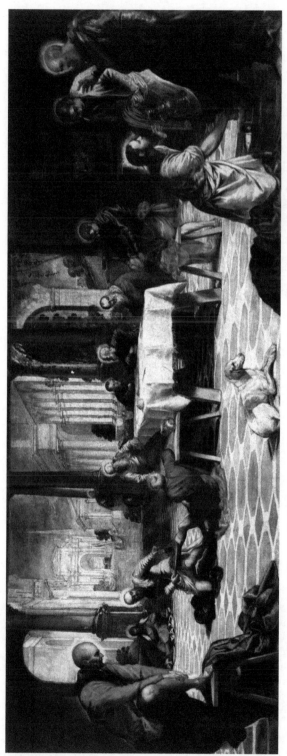

Fig. 02. Jacopo Robusti called Tintoretto. *Christ Washing the Disciples' Feet* (ca. 1547). PD Wikimedia Commons.

Tintoretto's controversial relationship with the *Scuole Grande* is well documented but he appears to have had an easier relationship with the guild and parish based *scuole*. Of the six versions of *Christ Washing His Disciples' Feet* painted by Tintoretto, four were painted for *Scuole del Sacramento*. By accepting commissions for parish-based *scuole*, Tintoretto would certainly have been aware of the humbler social circumstances of the membership to which he was addressing his paintings. It also seems to be that both Titian and Veronese painted one or, in the case of Veronese, may be two works for such confraternities as opposed to thirty or more by Tintoretto. Clearly, Tintoretto's emphasis on the humble circumstances of the people to whom Jesus addressed his earthly ministry would have been attractive to such parish groups. There were, therefore, business incentives for populating his works with unsophisticated or comic characters. However, when looking at Tintoretto's painting for San Marcuolo—*Christ Washing His Disciples' Feet*—it is difficult to avoid the impression that he enjoys their company. The portrayal is full of good humor. We are not sure how to respond: it rather depends upon which aspect of the painting we are looking at. What I think we do sense is what Freedberg refers to as Tintoretto's "radical's unrest."[18] First of all, where on earth are we? Classical arches and fishing boats in the background appear wholly out of place. And of course they are unless we change our mode of thought from the realism of the man on the floor having his leggings pulled off—an incident that would not be out of place in Shakespeare's Boar's Head Inn—to the blatant artificiality of a theatrical setting. Sebastiano Serlio (1474–1554) was an Italian Renaissance architect. He was a theoretician of theatrical scene design who developed standard settings for the various theatrical genres. What Tintoretto adopts in this painting is the cyclorama that Serlio prescribed for tragedies. The perspective lines of the back scene draw the viewer into the painting of what is now signaled as the scene from a tragic performance where we are confronted with low-life comedy. I think that it is appropriate to approach the paintings of Tintoretto as we would approach

18. Freedberg, *Painting in Italy*, 333.

a dramatic performance. A suggestion proposed by John Dixon might be useful at this point. Dixon takes a postmodern stance suggesting that the analysis of a work of art is "a reciprocation, dialogue, discourse, intercourse where the self, or all the participant selves, and the work of art are mutually defined."[19] We are participating or responding as members of an audience reacting to the interaction of the characters on a carefully arranged stage that uses theatrical techniques such as lighting, positioning, and gesture to convey understanding. As a way to encourage such a response I shall use stage directions when writing about the paintings.[20] If we imagine the painting *in situ* along the lateral stage-left wall of the *San Marcuolo* altar, the disciple extreme stage-right when we look at the painting frontally is taken to an extreme upstage position. This further isolates the figure, thought to be Judas, as he dries his feet reflecting upon what he is about to do. This positioning adds a note of great poignancy to the presentation. As members of the congregation, we would enter the painting, where Christ is convincing the confused Peter of the necessity of participation— "If I wash thee not, thou hast no part with me."[21] Between Christ and Peter, clasping the jug of water and a towel stands John. His head is bowed; his hair is disarrayed; his hands are clasped. His face and attitude are of deep reverential humility. In a vertical line above Christ's head, there is a background scene of *The Last Supper*. Tintoretto brings these two scenes together within the one painting emphasizing the theological connection and adding to the solemnity of the moment demonstrated by the figure of John. We see upstage-right of the painting another disciple who echoes this solemnity as he sits beneath a pillar, his hands clasped in prayer. To his stage-left, leaning in to him with the effort of pulling off a fellow disciple's leggings is the representation of the busyness

19. Dixon, John W. Jr. "Painting as Theological Thought the Issues in Tuscan Theology," http://www.unc.edu/~jwdixon/articles/tuscan.html, part ii

20. Directions refer to the characters in the drama rather than the viewer: stage left and right are to the left and right of the characters in the painting; upstage is to the back perspective and downstage is to the forward perspective.

21. John 13:8 (KJV).

of life that Christ has visited and sanctified. The smile that might come to the lips of the viewer at the ungainly attitude of the central pair thus becomes the utterance of a prayer. The painting may be divided vertically into three sections. Looking frontally, we have betrayal, prayer, and mundanity to our stage-right; somber reflection stage-center; divine humility, and human frailty stage-left. Downstage-center we have a dog: a faithful dog. The painting may be thus divided. But it would be very much diminished if it were. It stands as a magnificent panorama of the spiritual life as experienced by recognizable humanity. Serlio's cyclorama, prescribed for tragedy is finally seen to be appropriate as we, the viewers, know what human frailty is about, at its cost, to do.

In 1561, Tintoretto painted his version of *The Marriage at Cana* for the refectory of *The Monastery of the Crociferi*[22] in Cannaregio, Venice.

---

22. A Crucifer was one who carried a cross.

Fig. 03. Jacopo Robusti called Tintoretto. *The Marriage at Cana* (1561) courtesy of Ufficio Beni Culturali Diocesi Patriacarto di Venezia.

It is now to be seen in all its magnificence in the sacristy of *Santa Maria della Salute,* Venice. Please add it to your places to visit whilst in Venice. The Monastery housed a hospital that provided shelter and aid to pilgrims and crusaders on their way to the holy land Clearly, then, the requirement was for an inspirational painting to contemplate during the mealtime respite. The striking thing about this painting is that it is full of anecdotal detail, "full" being the operative word. There is plenty of incident to contemplate here. The concept of visual presentation as drama develops in Renaissance Venice into cinematic proportions. On the stage of a theatre the scene would be too "busy" to be coherent, but it seems to me that here we are presented with complexity and clarity at the same time. At the viewer/participator's entrance to the painting, we are confronted with the six amphorae. The original diners for whom it was intended, on their way to fight and likely to die for the faith could not miss the major theological theme of the wine of the New Covenant upon which that faith is based. It is in the light of that theme that the painting asks to be viewed. Once this is understood, the eye of the viewer is able to take on the role of a modern day cine camera and is able to pick out salient detail in a contemplative act. The perspective of the table leads us to the figures of Christ and Mary vaguely delineated at its head. The light that emanates from them identifies them for us but nobody within the painting focuses attention upon them. Everyone at the table is engaged in casual chat. There is a pervading sense of patient waiting. The man center-stage right of the table casually holds out an empty glass as he listens to the point being emphasized by the man next to him. The two females opposite are captured, arms folded, making melancholy conversation with the one positioned downstage lost in her somber reflection; her red nose and flushed cheek together with the modest attire are indicative of the humble social status that is shared by the rest of the guests. Ostentation and formal etiquette are missing. The leading participants in the gospel story are deliberately de-emphasized here. They merge into the ambience of the setting. This de-emphasizing of the physical presentation of Christ is to be seen in many of Tintoretto's paintings, particularly noticeable in the cycle of paintings for *The Scuola Grande di San Rocco*. This adds to the sense of historical narrative although the setting is brought forward. Tintoretto makes no attempt to contextualize the event to its historical setting. The political situation of contemporary Venice with its empire and trading position with Asia and the colorful exoticism associated with it is very clearly evoked. The turbans and fezzes, a familiar daily sight for Tintoretto—as recorded in the sculpture to be seen today in the *Piazza dei Mori*—are here in abundance. Oriental musical instruments are being played, the eastern custom of carrying heavy weights on the head is portrayed, and there is energy, vitality, and purpose everywhere contrasting with the casual waiting at the table. The heft of the amphora down-left and the muscularity of the arms that grasp it are palpable. But there is emptiness and want at the entrance to the painting. This is poignantly conveyed by the woman in the foreground whose head is highlighted against the whiteness of the tablecloth over which she leans. Her glass bowl is empty as are all the vessels on the table. The amphora to which she advances her glass is empty also. The glass is in a direct perspective line with the figure of Christ which makes a very clear point, elegantly and unobtrusively: it is to the men with the empty vessel that attention is turned within the painting. Mary points out to Jesus, the Gospel tells us, "They have no wine." The three downstage-center females behind the woman holding out her glass appear to be rather amusedly intrigued: they focus on the water being poured from the held amphora into the one on the floor rather like three members of a modern audience invited onto the stage following the odd instructions of a conjurer. The central one doesn't quite know where to position her glass. Is the water going to change to wine mid-stream? These are the knowing servants and it's all a bit of a lark. Tintoretto's controversial *prestezza*[23] is very effective here. The material world of costumes and faces is suggested rather than realized in elaborate detail, particularly in the distant presentation of Christ and Mary. The dress of the female figure holding out her glass expectantly downstage center is represented with a

23. See note 8 *intro.*

few rapid, impatient brush strokes or dabs even. But the gesture and movement running right across the front of the painting are perfectly realized. Moving from stage-left to right we have physical effort, expectation, want, helplessness. It is an abbreviated human saga. The transient nature of this saga is conveyed by the fragility of the manner in which the characters are painted. They certainly look as if they are "such stuff as dreams are made on."[24] The three characters surrounding the Ionic pillar upstage-center-right are fading into the material behind them. There is no suggestion that these are anything but good honest people happy in each other's company. But there is something lacking: the fruit of the vine. The transformation taking place downstage-center is, the painting suggests, about to change all that.

24. Shakespeare, *The Tempest*.

# 1

# THE SCUOLA GRANDE
# DI SAN ROCCO

*The Scuola Grande di San Rocco* comprises three rooms:

a) Sala Terrena—Lower Room.

b) Sala Superiore—Upper Room.

c) Sala dell' Albergo—of prime importance as charitable mission headquarters.

In 1564, there was a competition amongst the leading painters of Venice for the commission to decorate the *Sala dell'Albergo* in the Scuola. According to Vasari, Tintoretto carried out something of a coup. The rivals were asked to submit designs of their proposed work. Tintoretto placed a finished work of the apotheosis of Saint Roch, *Saint Roch in Glory*, in the central ceiling panel of the Albergo and offered it as a gift to the fraternity. Clearly, this did nothing to endear him to his fellow artists. Tintoretto's sophistication in interpreting and exploiting the situation to his own advantage can be seen when looking at the panel itself. The allusion to Titian's *Assumption of the Virgin* in the neighboring *Santa Maria Gloriosa dei Frari* was clearly intended to appeal to and placate the conservative tastes of the brothers.[1] In spite of the formal complexity,[2] the reference to the master —Titian—with the tunic of the Saint painted in the red of the gown of Titian's Virgin, was calculated to calm the suspicions of the most antagonistic brother regarding Tintoretto's innovative style. Even so, Tintoretto won the competition by a fairly narrow margin of votes and he became, rather controversially, the official painter of the *Sala dell'Albergo*. His scheme seems to have worked and his decoration of the *Albergo* was warmly approved. Those fortunate enough to have visited Tintoretto's magnificent version of the Crucifixion have cause to be very grateful for that.

In 1565, Tintoretto was welcomed into the confraternity and quickly rose to influential status on the ruling committee. Although receiving commissions to produce paintings for the Scuola's church, it was another decade before, in 1575, Tintoretto's offer to paint the ceiling of the Scuola's *Sala Superiore* was accepted. Later, he offered to produce three paintings per year until the whole *Sala Superiore* was decorated with narrative wall paintings by his hand. He requested one hundred ducats a year for life in return. This was accepted and the work was completed in 1581. He went on to complete paintings for the *Sala Terrena* in 1587. But he remained a controversial choice with nearly half the confraternity voting against him in 1578.

> At his death in 1594, the total cost of Tintoretto's paintings for the Meeting House (including those in the Albergo and inclusive of expenses) was little more than 2,000 ducats.[3]

This is approximately the price Titian reportedly commanded for just one painting. Given Tintoretto's association with the *poligrafi*[4] circle, he was likely to have been sympathetic to the criticism of the perceived backsliding of the Scuole and keen to encourage a

1. Take a look: it's just a few steps across the piazza.
2. Now referred to as mannerist.
3. Nichols, *Tradition*, 176.
4. See note 4 *intro*.

more spiritual outlook. The order of work was dictated by the importance of the rooms for the confraternity. The Sala dell'Albergo was of prime importance as it was the room in which the officers of the government of the Scuola met to discuss and determine the management and direction of their charitable mission. The Sala Superiore is the main meeting house, perhaps comparable to the chapter house of a cathedral. The Sala Terrena is the entrance hall. I shall approach the paintings as a modern day visitor which, of course, I am. My visit culminates with the Sala dell' Albergo and Tintoretto's magnificent *Crucifixion*. This seems to be entirely appropriate as the final Word of Tintoretto's contribution to the Scuola's continuing mission.

In 1555, the Scuola had been given Titian's *Annunciation* as a bequest in the will of Melio da Cortona. He was a *condottiere*[5] and general of the Venetian Republic. The gift was highly prized by the Scuola and it was displayed as dictated by the will in a frame emblazoned with the da Cortona coat of arms on the high wall over the landing on the grand staircase. It therefore greeted Tintoretto on his way to work in the Sala dell' Albergo and the Sala Superiore each morning. One can only imagine the memories of Tintoretto's less than cordial relationship with the venerated master painter that were evoked as he passed under the painting on a daily basis. Also, he may have reflected upon the often less than favorable comparisons of his work with that of the master that he had to tolerate. But more importantly, I suspect that Tintoretto sympathized with the criticism that the Scuola had to endure regarding its cultivation of such socially elevated people as the donor Melio de Cortona causing it to lose sight of its founding humble dedication to the poor and disadvantaged members of Venetian society. In 1588, Tintoretto's *Visitation* was commissioned as a pendant over the opposite archway on the same landing as Titian's painting. Today, both paintings smile at one another over the landing in their original positions. RIP little dyer.

---

5. Italian captains of contracted mercenary companies. *Condotta* =contract.

# 2

# THE SALA TERRENA.

The ground-floor entrance-hall was obviously more than that terminology suggests. It has a large altar at the far end and also a statue of Saint Roch. It was clearly used for liturgical services as well as gatherings of the brotherhood and their family and visitors. As previously stated, Tintoretto decorated the walls of this room at the end of his work at the Scuola. However, the subject matter of the paintings anticipates those already completed in that they deal with the Incarnation, the life of Mary, and the childhood of Christ whereas the upper-floor paintings deal with Christ's life and passion. Scholarly investigation suggests that Tintoretto may have been aided by assistants in these lower-room paintings, in particular by his son Domenico. However, the hand of Jacopo is clearly recognized as having had the major input.

Fig. 04. Jacopo Robusti called Tintoretto *The Annunciation* (1583–87) with gratitude for the generosity of the *Scuola Grande di San Rocco*.

## The Sala Terrena.

The first painting to greet the visitor to their left of the entrance is the very impressive *Annunciation*. Tintoretto, of course, was very well aware not only of Titian's international reputation but, in particular, the reverence in which he was held by the brotherhood, greatly treasuring the *Annunciation* of Titian under which Tintoretto had daily passed for many years. Many of the brothers appeared to have been rather uneasy about the work of the man chosen to decorate the walls of their Scuola. Now, here was this man brazenly asking them to look at his aggressively challenging version of a sacred subject alongside, as it were, of the elegantly-finished work by the High Renaissance master just up the stairs. The airborne invasion of Tintoretto's Gabriel clearly references the presentation of the angel in Titian's work. If this was intended to placate Tintoretto's critics, it seems to me that it would have had the opposite effect. The environment that is invaded by Tintoretto's Gabriel is literally a world away from that of Titian. It is aggressively of this world. Titian's is at a spiritual remove from this world: it calms where Tintoretto's disturbs. The clutter and the disarray suggests that the angel is addressing someone in a ruined and abandoned building that at one time was proudly palatial. The painting is fronted with a dilapidated pillar the facing of which is disintegrating to reveal the basic brickwork underneath. Stage-right of this is makeshift workshop with a carpenter, supposedly Joseph,[1] working at a bench. There is a wicker chair in need of repair. That such a presentation was accepted by the Scuola at all may perhaps be explained by the fact that it was a community that was sensitive to the demands made by the Council of Trent for evangelical reform. Particular emphasis had been placed upon the association between material poverty and inner grace. Józef Grabski[2] draws our attention to the splendor of the ceiling above the Virgin in Tintoretto's painting and likens it to that of the main meeting hall of the brotherhood on the floor above. He convincingly goes on to suggest that the ruined column raised on a pedestal

---

1. The youthful figure has been suggested as Christ in a mystical future projection.

2. Grabski, "The Group of Paintings by Tintoretto in the 'Sala Terrena.'"

that divides Tintoretto's painting is very similar to columns in the *Sala Terrena* itself and the tiled floor in the painting could be an extension of the floor of the *Sala Terrena*. Tintoretto reminds his viewers, ancient and modern, that treasure on earth corrupts. We should focus on that which is incorruptible.

**Fig. 05.** Jacopo Robusti called Tintoretto. *The Adoration of the Magi* (1582) with gratitude for the generosity of the *Scuola Grande di San Rocco*.

*The Adoration of the Magi* is of great interest positioned as it is next to *The Annunciation* where Tintoretto has been seen to emphasize the poverty and humility of the setting with comparative suggestions of the splendor within which the Scuola has embedded itself. The Adoration of the Magi had frequently been chosen by wealthy patrons throughout the Renaissance as a subject that would allow painters to flamboyantly demonstrate the patron's wealth and attendant position in society. Kings, crowns, splendid robes, attendants, and retinues gave ample opportunity for this. To some extent, it might be rather difficult to avoid a rather sharp contrast to Tintoretto's "shocking" *Annunciation*. However, Tintoretto establishes the tone with a very distant picture of galloping horses bearing military-looking persons. The leaping dog adds a sense of some activity. Maybe they are the retinue of the Magi, maybe Herod's soldiers. Whoever they are they are painted in a subdued manner. There is a ghostly unreality about them. They are from an "unreal" world. In comparison to the brightly-shining world of the Christ child pinpointed by the light of the star above, they do not merit the painter's attention. The two magi who are bareheaded and kneeling represent the power of the church in Rome and that of the state in Venice paying homage to a child. The central kneeling figure on the raised platform is adorned with a doge-like ermine cape. The kneeling figure stage-left of the platform with his arms spread in adulation wears the robes of a prince of the church. The stooping central magus is about to lay his gift on the platform before the child. He retains his crown as a symbol of royalty to dignify the gift after which he will, as his associating magi have done, remove it to signify his personal abasement before the child. There is bare brick and rough wood symbolism that is carried through to the first painting in the upstairs room, *The Adoration of the Shepherds*. But it is the characters that front *The Adoration of the Magi* that most clearly indicate Tintoretto's thematic consistency. Joseph stands to the stage-right of the platform. He leans forward to stare fixedly at the mystery of the child's presence a cross between a proud father and a perplexed servant. There is a unique diversity of characters that the painter associates with the elevated oriental royalty. Downstage-right, her left hand clutching her breast in awe, a young woman has brought an offering of two doves. This is the offering of the poor that Luke[3] tells us Mary and Joseph brought to the temple presentation of Jesus. It is this downstage-center offering that Tintoretto features not the magnificence of the gold, frankincense and myrrh with which we are all familiar. It immediately sets up a direct association between the poor worshiper and the holy mother situated directly above her within the painting. On the extreme stage-left another poor woman with a basket of offerings enters from behind the brick pillar. In front of her the semi-naked figure of a man stretching out a string of beads in offering is seen. His head is partly shaved and he has the appearance of a native American, the recently discovered race and a subject of the post-Trent evangelizing mission. Wealthy late sixteenth-century patrons were probably not yet ready for him and perhaps this was the point of Tintoretto's inclusion.

3. Luke 2:24.

Fig. 06. Jacopo Robusti called Tintoretto. *The Flight into Egypt* (1582–87) with gratitude for the generosity of the *Scuola Grande di San Rocco.*

*The Flight into Egypt* presents the Holy Family heading out of the downstage-right corner of the painting. This break with the traditional representation of the Holy Family traversing across the surface of the painting immediately indicates the independent approach that Tintoretto brings to his *Scuola di San* Rocco work. Evidently, the painting was positioned so that the bench beneath it to which the holy refugees appear to be heading was the position where the poor of Venice waited for the charity of the brotherhood. Again, Tintoretto reminds the Scuola that their founding commitment was to the poor and needy and in fulfilling the commitment they were doing it unto God. But there is a unity to the approach that Tintoretto makes to his subject matter so that it is not limited to the form of a mere didactic lesson. Nature provides a sheltering embrace around the group. The stage-right tree overarches the nursing mother protectively and the palm-tree extreme stage-left is suggestive of Egypt, the destination of the travellers. The symbolism that surrounds this forwardly sheltered grouping is unobtrusively accessible. The downstage-right figure of Joseph and the donkey is particularly poignant. Joseph is bent in irritable agitation; the donkey is bent, head dropped in fatigue, in humble submission; they are attached by a carefully-drawn looped rope. Poor old Joseph, so much is demanded of him in the passion narrative. Poor old donkey, he has to bear the new-born savior to wearisome safety and later to bear him back again to crucifixion.[4] The rope borne between them is a reminder of the rope that binds Jesus before his tormentors. Downstage-left there is a rough-hewn inescapable cross. Downstage-center there are the accouterments of the poor traveller. It is a deeply-moving presentation. This is enhanced by the surrounding background. To the upper stage-right of the Virgin's head in the far distance is what is likely to be Jerusalem. On the opposite side of the trees, upstage-left is further evidence of unwelcoming civilization. The closer background

---

4. Obviously, I refer not to this particular representative of the "universal donkey" (cf. Keats' nightingale). One can imagine this donkey reflecting with Puck in Shakespeare's *A Midsummer Night's Dream*, "Lord, what fools these mortals be!"

stage-left shows a scene of peasant subsistence labor separated by what we have seen as the protecting thicket. From this new perspective, the thicket appears as an impenetrable barrier to their salvation. It is not a painting to calm viewers/participators with the serenity of "all will be well" but one that suggests there is much work to be done, starting with each one of us: the profound council of Trent message.

**Fig. 07.** Jacopo Robusti called Tintoretto. *The Massacre of the Innocents* (1582–87) with gratitude for the generosity of the *Scuola Grande di San Rocco.*

The rough-cross motif in the extreme downstage-left position of *The Flight into Egypt* is very poignantly positioned next to *The Massacre of the Innocents* on the wall of *Sala Terrena*. It leads us visually from a scene featuring the tranquil embrace of a natural setting to one featuring the harsh classical lines of man's ordering. It is used by Tintoretto as a bitterly ironical setting for the utter chaos of the violently dramatic and heart-rending *Massacre*. We viewers/participators move from a lovingly detailed and colored world to harsh, dry-brushed world of sketchy, colorless and soulless, man-made hell. It is within, and over, and out-of this heartless shell that Herod's evil is hatched. The figure groupings with which we are confronted present monumental variations on the theme of unadulterated male brutality: the attempt to annihilate the *caritas*[5] that is symbolized throughout the cycle of the *Scuola's* paintings by bare-breasted nursing mothers. However, there is a central allusion to the triumphal *caritas* of the Crucifixion: Tom Nichols draws our attention to the stage-center image of a mother staring at her dead child stretched out in front of her "in the manner of a *Pietà*."[6] A dead or dying woman leans over the wall upstage-right, desperately clinging to her naked and doomed child. To her stage-left, in sharp contrast, a male pushes a dead woman over the edge of the wall, ripping the child to which she has clung in her death throes from her embrace to certain death. Difficult as it is to give these events words, one can only imagine the overwhelming passion of the man giving them an image. Tintoretto has depicted seemingly endless individual dramas fading into the far distance. Upstage-left, through the archway, there is a very fine example of Tintoretto's purposeful use of the *prestezza* for which he was often maligned. It is a vaguely painted yet unmistakably moving image of *caritas*. Literally in the middle of the utter chaos in front and behind them to which they must inevitably succumb, there is a vision of great tenderness presented as contrastingly inevitable: one

5. A Latin word for which I can find no modern equivalent. It is variously translated as *charity, caring, love,* all of which have become tarnished. See "Concluding Remarks."

6. Nichols, *Tradition,* 224.

woman surrenders her child to the caring arms of another clearly intending to convey it to safety.

The image is difficult to see but it is there and Tintoretto's technique captures that truth of a sometimes almost untraceable human lovingkindness[7]. The woman downstage-right holds a bloody knife in her right hand won we may suppose in a clearly unsuccessful struggle as her child is wrenched from her weakened left arm. Opposite, downstage-left, a soldier in a vermillion cloak makes an energetic, violent flourish as he surveys the scene.

---

7. "Lovingkindness" is the English translation of the Hebrew word "chesed." It is used frequently in the book of Psalms. It describes divine love.

Fig. 08. Jacopo Robusti called Tintoretto. *The Massacre of the Innocents* (detail) PD Wikimedia Commons.

## The Sala Terrena.

*The Circumcision of Christ* is regarded as the work of Domenico, the son of Tintoretto. It is of considerable interest to compare *the Circumcision of Christ* by Domenico with *The Adoration of the Magi* by his father on the opposite wall upon which the arrangement of Domenico's painting is clearly based. Tom Nichols is very helpful here:

> Despite working in the Tintorettesque idiom, he [Domenico] modifies it to a display of luxuriant surface and texture underpinned by careful finish and studied composition. . . . it is as if the son himself wished to answer the ringing charges made against his father, seeking to normalize a style which for many art connoisseurs seemed merely a product of eccentricity.[8]

The detailed attention to costume and faces tells us that instead of being invited to participate in the challenging world of a unique imagination we are being asked to look at a world very similar to our own.

8. Nichols, *Tradition*, 228.

Fig. 09. Jacopo Robusti called Tintoretto. *The Circumcision* (1587) with gratitude for the generosity of the *Scuola Grande di San Rocco.*

Given that the paintings of the *Sala Terrena* have focused on the Incarnation and, therefore, the central role of Mary in Redemption Theology and the doctrinal energy of The Council of Trent, *The Assumption of the Virgin* is appropriately positioned as we ascend to the next level of paintings focusing on the life and passion of Christ. The painting has suffered much damage and restoration over the years. However, there is a vibrant energy and imaginative penetration about it that excites and tells us that the master is involved. I referred to Titian's famous work on the same subject in the neighboring *Basilica di Santa Maria Gloriosa dei Frari* when writing about Tintoretto's first commission at *The Scuola Grande di San Rocco* in 1564. Quite clearly, Tintoretto alludes to Titian's work here also. But there is a wonderful touch that apart from anything else would act as Tintoretto's signature on the painting. Otherworldly though the evocation certainly is, Tintoretto unites it with our own world. The tomb from which the Virgin ascends is incorporated within the top frame of the door through which we pass to the upper room. The angelic *putto* assisting the Virgin's rise adds purchase to his upward thrust by throwing his pudgy little leg over the top of our door. One doesn't really associate Tintoretto with a sense of humor, but he had to be smiling when he came up with that one!

Fig. 10. Jacopo Robusti called Tintoretto. *The Assumption of the Virgin* (1582–97) with gratitude for the generosity of the *Scuola Grande di San Rocco.*

*The Sala Terrena.*

Finally, when approaching the altar to give thanks and ask for a blessing before continuing one's visit whether that purpose be to assemble for business in the *Sala Superiore* or the *Sala dell' Albergo* or, in modern times, simply to view and participate in the paintings, one is blessed by two beautiful paintings of the utmost serenity.

Fig. 11. Jacopo Robusti called Tintoretto. *Female Saint Reading in a Landscape* (1582–87) with gratitude for the generosity of the *Scuola Grande di San Rocco.*

**Fig. 12. Jacopo Robusti called Tintoretto.** *Female Saint Reading in a Landscape* (1582–87) with gratitude for the generosity of the *Scuola Grande di San Rocco.*

One is in the corner to the left of the altar and the other in the opposite corner to the right of the altar. They are both titled *Female Saint Reading in a Landscape*. Figure 11 has been identified as Saint Mary Magdalene and figure 12 as Saint Mary of Egypt but many remain unconvinced by these identifications. I, personally, warm to the idea that they are both depictions of the Virgin Mary as, apart from anything else, from *The Annunciation* through to *The Assumption of the Virgin* it is she who has been prominently featured in Tintoretto's paintings of the Redemption Narrative. However, the emphasis of both paintings is not upon the figures but upon the landscapes. These are both bathed in a beautiful golden light that gives them a visionary quality. We are not looking at objective reality indeed the saint in figure 11 is not even looking at the scenery. What is being shared is that which has been inspired by the holy book that she reads. The hugely naked bole of a large tree stretches out in front of her. Lit luminously and with large arms outstretched it rises from the earth dwarfing her presence without in any way alarming her. Her left hand is completely relaxed as is the arm and hand with which she holds her book. The specter of the tree clearly alludes to the Crucifixion but what she reads presents it in a manner that calms her. As evening falls, she is assured that all is well. The opposite painting has the saint lifting her eyes from the book. What her reading has inspired is a unique understanding of her natural environment. She sees a magical vision of a palm tree and its surrounding trees highlighted against the evening sky. She looks towards what might be a vision of Jerusalem where the consummation of the redemption narrative is to take place. To "see" all this in the golden glow of a balmy evening surrounded by a fertile and gently watered landscape is to recall the words of the Psalmist:

Be still and know that I am God.[9]

Nature has been invaded and transformed by *the Word*. What Tintoretto presents us with is the mystical theology of the Incarnation.

9. Ps 46:10 (KJV).

# 3

## THE SALA SUPERIORE

Fig. 13. Jacopo Robusti called Tintoretto. *The Adoration of the Shepherds* (1578–81) with gratitude for the generosity of the *Scuola Grande di San Rocco.*

Nichols sees the spiritual intensity of Tintoretto's work being developed within the paintings of the *Scuola Grande di San Rocco*. Within this context, the first painting in the left-hand corner of the facing wall as one enters from the stairway (figure 13) is rather surprising. There is certainly a tone of traditional humility conveyed by the central presentation of the animals. But the detailed, naturalistic picture of the rustic setting is what immediately strikes the viewer. However, it becomes increasingly difficult to avoid a sense that the humble setting, very poor materially, is being presented as a place of sanctity: the sense of poverty merges with that of holiness to become one idea. The two shepherds downstage-right seem to render the act of giving into a stately pas de deux. The two older shepherds downstage-left gaze in reverence with prayerful hands. The downstage-center trio of ox, hen, and peacock have all their symbolic attachments subsumed into an act of humble worship. Upper stage-left, the Holy Family are arranged and lit iconically, with Mary delicately revealing her brightly-lit child to the two serving maids stage-right. The further right of the two maids is preparing baby-pap with a spoon. Her exposed breast reveals her traditional wet-nurse role although perhaps redundant on this occasion and simply symbolizing the spirit of charity.

> The *Adoration of the Shepherds* ... features a wet nurse ... Tintoretto knew, of course, that the nursing of Christ was the undisputed prerogative of the *Madonna Lactans*.[1]

The overall lighting is very dramatically effective with the *pas de deux shepherds* counterpoised in light and shadow. These effects suggest that the initial naturalistic impression is actually charged with a subtle spirituality. What, for example, is to be seen shedding light through the rough wooden beams? Is this a reference as in *The Ascension* downstairs to the splendidly sumptuous ceiling of the *Sala Superiore* under which the membership, according to their critics, were being seduced away from their mission of humility and charitable giving. Maybe Tintoretto in his painting is showing us the glory the sight of which might be obscured by riches.

---

1. Sperling, "Allegories of Charity," 129.

At the time Tintoretto was working within The *Scuola Grande di San Rocco* twenty percent of the Venetian population were estimated to be paupers. Single women in particular single mothers were among the most vulnerable at the time. Abandoned pregnant women were a rapidly increasing focus of charitable giving. Legacies to provide dowries so that marriages restoring honor to such paupers might be arranged seem to have had popular appeal for the pious. It was not uncommon for single mothers to sell their milk. Within this context, the bare-breasted serving maid with two associates and a group of poor shepherds welcoming the birth of Christ tells us much regarding Tintoretto's sympathies upon the basis of which *The Scuola* was founded: a fact of which they may be in need of regular recall.

Fig. 14. Jacopo Robusti called Tintoretto. *The Prayer in the Garden* (1578–81) with gratitude for the generosity of the *Scuola Grande di San Rocco*.

*The Prayer in the Garden* is set in the Garden of Gethsemane on the Mount of Olives. Gethsemane in Hebrew is *gat shemanim* that translates as oil press. Tintoretto uses a very ancient form of the *Mandorla*.[2] This surrounding of light is found in fifth century mosaics in the West usually surrounding the figure of Christ. It is a form derived from the eastern iconic tradition and by surrounding his *mandorla* with olives, Tintoretto makes a powerful symbolic allusion to Christ's imminent redemptive shedding of blood as the olive is pressed to release its substance. The moment depicted is that recorded in the Gospel of Matthew.

> And he went a little farther, and fell on his face, and prayed, saying, O my Father, if it be possible, let this cup pass from me: nevertheless not as I will, but as thou wilt.[3]

However, Christ is not depicted as collapsing in prayer as Matthew suggests. Christ appears to be sleeping. The energetic invasion of the angel upstage-left recalls depictions of the Annunciation where Gabriel announces God's plan to Mary. Just as Mary was required to accept the will of God to bring his son into our world, so Jesus is required to accept his father's consummation of that plan. The "cup" sanctified by a halo of light has powerful eucharistic overtones for the viewer/participator. In the light of the mandorla, the dimly lit advancing soldiers appear , literally, faintly ridiculous. They creep along, heavily armed with their leader's outstretched arms suggesting that he is struggling not to overbalance and reveal their presence before they have secured their quarry. The supernatural light from above creates a warm glow highlighting the human huddle of the three apostles below stage-left. The youthful John's serenely sleeping face contrasts humorously with the bald head of an older man catching the holy light like a brightly shining moon. There is a magnificent triumphant note sounded that dominates a choral presentation of profound agony. There is human arrogant stupidity, human warmth and humor. Life.

2. Italian: almond.
3. Matt 26:39 (KJV).

Fig. 15. Jacopo Robusti called Tintoretto. *The Last Supper* (1579–81) with gratitude for the generosity of the *Scuola Grande di San Rocco.*

In *The Last Supper* Tintoretto creates a sense of depth, setting the central table diagonally to the picture frame. This enables him to employ perspective very effectively. At the downstage-left and downstage-right points of the viewer/participant's entry points we have a male and a female beggar. They form the base of a right-angled triangle. The bread at the side of the male and the wine by the female presents them as taking part in the eucharistic moment. The upright of the triangle is formed by taking the base from the head of the male beggar to the head of Christ almost at the vanishing perspective point. The sheer audacity of the statement that Tintoretto makes here is quite stunning and one can imagine the discomfort of some of the brotherhood trying to come to terms with it. Perhaps it might recall the Last Judgment teaching of Jesus as recorded in Matthew's gospel.

> . . . Inasmuch as ye have done it unto one of the least of these my brethren, ye have done it unto me.[4]

And perhaps this recall would cause the brotherhood to reflect upon the criticism that was current regarding their loss of focus upon the humility and charity of their founding mission. Within the painting, the beggar is more prominent than Christ. It is almost as if he, in fact, becomes Christ and that Tintoretto presents a profoundly spiritual proposition that Christ is the beggar pleading for our aid. The humility of the scene is evident. The apostles are barefoot and kneeling or arranged unceremoniously around a table set in a rather monumental space rendered low-key with a kitchen background in which "local" Venetians go about their business in a very relaxed manner. Tintoretto shows the light as coming from two sources, one in front of the scene and one behind to the stage-left of the kitchen. The highlights and shadows thus created contribute to the sense of energetic activity. This is not an inwardly meditating group. They are excitedly, agitatedly discussing, interrupting, talking over one another apart from poor old John who is overcome. He is almost impossible to see in prints, asleep on the lap of Jesus. In fact, Tintoretto paints him almost as

4. Matt 25:40 (KJV).

an integral part of Christ. He is at one with Christ. The key moment of the painting where Christ establishes the sacrament of the Eucharist is placed at the vanishing perspective area of the painting. Christ offers the bread (anachronistically depicted as a wafer by Tintoretto) to Peter with the words,

> This is my body which is given for you: this do in remembrance of me.[5]

This is a prelude to the Crucifixion, the cosmic act of charitable humility. In order to arrive at it visually we have to negotiate the figure of a half-naked beggar. This suggests that Tintoretto is anxious that his viewers/participators should not be allowed to retreat into litany.[6]

The spiritual intensity that Nichols sees as being developed in Tintoretto's work at *the Scuola Grande di San Rocco* is best observed if paintings are placed in context rather than studied in isolation. I choose *The Raising of Lazarus* as the focal point of Tintoretto's work on the opposite west wall as the narrative is often regarded as the prefiguring of The Resurrection. It is The Resurrection towards which the spiritual intensity of the work of Tintoretto drives and from which it emanates. Dostoevsky, writing in the nineteenth century, presents the narrative of *The Raising of Lazarus* at a critical point of chapter four in his novel *Crime and Punishment*. Raskolnikov is a murderer and Sonia is a prostitute. They have reached the depth of human degradation and despair. Sonia reads to Raskolnikov the whole passage from John's Gospel relating the story of Lazarus. At the end of her reading, Dostoevsky writes a sentence that carries an energy beyond that of a simple narrative description. It presents a vision of the unaccommodated human condition:

> The candle-end was flickering out in the battered candlestick, dimly lighting up in the poverty-stricken room

5. Luke 22:19 (KJV).

6. Cf. the positioning of the poor woman and her offering of two doves in relation to the figure of the Virgin in *The Adoration of the Magi* in the *Sala Terrena*.

the murderer and the harlot who had so strangely been reading together the eternal book. Five minutes or more passed.

We have poverty, restricted vision, degradation, and the Gospel. It seems to me that Tintoretto presents the Gospel in his paintings energized by a similar vision. I propose to view Tintoretto's *The Raising of Lazarus* in relation to the works placed either side of it in the Sala Superiore.

Fig. 16. Jacopo Robusti called Tintoretto. *The Miracle of the Loaves and Fishes* (1579–81) with gratitude for the generosity of the *Scuola Grande di San Rocco*.

To the stage-right is *The Miracle of the Loaves and Fishes*. The dark, shadowy foreground is contrasted with the background lit by a roseate sky at sunset. It is also illuminated by breast-feeding women. The angle of the hillside slope is paralleled by the placement of the three figures at the top of the hill. The Fourth Gospel relates[7] that Andrew, Simon Peter's brother, brings a boy to Jesus. The boy has a small supply of bread and fish, presumably for his own needs. This appears to be the moment depicted in Tintoretto's painting. Jesus is the stage-right character receiving the boy with Andrew to his stage-left. Both Andrew and Jesus appear to be coaxing the boy who is understandably rather bemused. This perplexity suggesting a fear of being "taken in" is humanly and regularly portrayed in paintings of individuals confronted by Jesus. Apprehensive perplexity might well be taken as a theme in such paintings irrespective of period or painter. It makes a very significant and reassuring contribution to our understanding of the demands made upon us by the Gospel two millennia hence. A very striking feature of this painting is that nobody in the surrounding crowd is looking at Jesus: they are all preoccupied with caring for one another. Whether it is the half-naked beggar reaching out for aid stage-center or the well-dressed family group downstage-left, they share one thing in common: human need. Upstage-left, highlighted against the bright sky, a mother breast-feeds her child. Another to her stage-right nurses two babies. These examples of the unconditional giving of oneself, or Charity, are prominent evangelical references in the work of Tintoretto. To the extreme stage-left of the painting, beneath the breast-feeding mother, a carefully delineated face watches the charitable activity approvingly. His gaze is directed towards the two figures downstage-right. One standing male figure tenderly hands a bowl of sustenance to a seated female figure. Everyone appears to be concerned for the wellbeing of his or her neighbor. Perhaps this watching figure, stage-left is a lay member of the fraternity reminding the painting's viewers or *participators* of their charitable obligation. In contrast to these charitable acts, highlighted at the back of the painting, the faces

7. John 6:8–9.

of Jesus and Andrew are silhouetted against the sky. The embodiment of *caritas*, the Word made flesh, is concealed. Charity is self-abnegating. The theme of the Eucharist, strongly re-emphasized by the Council of Trent, is clearly present here. This eucharistic theme is present throughout the cycle of paintings in the *Sala Superiore*. It culminates in the monumental "Crucifixion"—the archetypal act of *caritas*—in the adjoining *Sala dell' Albergo.*

Fig. 17. Jacopo Robusti called Tintoretto. *The Raising of Lazarus* (1579–81) with gratitude for the generosity of the *Scuola Grande di San Rocco.*

The immediately striking feature of *The Raising of Lazarus* to the stage-left of *The Miracle of the Loaves and Fishes* is the positioning of the figure of Christ downstage-left. If the silhouetted figure of Christ in the previous painting is obscured by shadow, the positioning of Christ to the margin of the present painting represents a variation of this lack of emphasis on the physical presence of Christ. Certainly, the dramatic gesture of Martha, directs our attention towards Christ. His face here is lit unlike that of the previous painting. However, it is the resurrected figure of Lazarus that is in the dominant position within the painting as he is helped from the tomb. The figure beneath Lazarus to his stage-left stares into his face as if to make sure that it is not some kind of a trick he is witnessing. If the event is understood to prefigure Christ's own resurrection, this figure might be taken as prefiguring Thomas who wants tactile evidence that Christ has really conquered death. But, in spite of the dominant position, the figure of Lazarus does not dominate the painting. A circular movement or visual energy rather like a whirlwind within the painting prevents this. Starting from the dramatically gesturing right hand of Christ that seems to illuminate the face and awed gesture of Martha, this energy moves upwards through the body of the figure stage-right of Lazarus. This figure strains on the winding sheet that serves as a hoist to lift the awakened Lazarus from his slumber. The movement tilts him forward. This carries the energy of the painting to the speculative figure below and returns it, via his pointing left hand to the figure of Christ. It is like perpetual motion that carries the question running throughout the Fourth Gospel: who is this man? We are not distracted by "the physical property of paint, its material *richezza* as (we) might be in a work by Titian or Veronese."[8] The harmonious color tones act like a spell over the whole work that is not broken by sharply delineated figures. Mary, upstage-right of Martha inhales a sweet-smelling balm, no doubt to avoid her contemplation being interrupted by the stench of death. Notwithstanding the dramatic and disturbing action being depicted, a sense of calm represented by the figure of Mary pervades the painting as if what

8. Nichols, *Tradition*, 212–14.

she holds dispenses intoxicating incense that sanctifies the occasion subduing an emotional response from the background figures upstage-left. The foliage is arranged in a very decorous fashion that dignifies as it poeticizes the presentation.

Fig. 18. Jacopo Robusti called Tintoretto. *The Ascension* (1579–81) with gratitude for the generosity of the *Scuola Grande di San Rocco.*

The dramatic contrast of *The Ascension* positioned as it is to the stage-left of *The Raising of Lazarus* is very striking. The figure of Christ triumphant dominates the painting. Born aloft on the wings of angels, Christ's focus is now upon his heavenly destination. Beneath him lies a desolate landscape. Whilst contrasting dramatically with the position of Christ in *The Raising of Lazarus* the painting connects with that in the ceiling oval above it: *Jacob's Ladder*.

Fig. 19. Jacopo Robusti called Tintoretto. *Jacob's Ladder* (1577–78) with gratitude for the generosity of the *Scuola Grande di San Rocco*.

Jacob sleeps at the bottom of the painting. The ladder with angels ascending and descending is clearly presented as a visionary experience. The ethereal quality of the painting is beautifully rendered. It is a tribute to the formal delicacy of which Tintoretto was capable. The painting emphasizes the vitality of individual spiritual experience in line with the priority given to the spirituality of the faithful by the Catholic Renewal Movement of the period. *The Ascension of Christ* extends this idea with the role of the figure of Jacob in the ceiling roundel being fulfilled by the apostle downstage-right in *The Ascension of Christ* as he reads his Bible with his back toward the subject matter of the painting. The idea conveyed is that such miraculous events are, or may be, a reality of inner contemplative experience. Against this higher positioned reality, the lower reality pales into insignificance. The two faint central figures on the lower plane have been identified as Moses and Elijah. These are historical figures whose finite earthly time has been superseded by eternal time. The Bible-reading foreground figure is given a strong visual presence that matches those above. Partaking of the Word of God. he, like them, becomes eternal.

The paintings in both the *Sala Terrena* and the *Sala Superiore* emphasize the themes of eucharistic piety and the confraternity's founding commitment to the poor that Caravia and others regarded as having been neglected. The brotherhood is also reminded of their commitment to *amor proximi*, the practical expression of their neighborly love. The great, triumphant *Ascension of Christ* underlines the visionary aspect of the cycle of paintings, an experience available to the faithful who follow the example of Christ's *humilitas* emphasized in the narrative paintings that precede it.

> The paintings are pregnant vehicles of religious experience, not just from their quality of illustration but from the presence in them of a power that infuses what is illustrated with spirituality.[9]

9. Freedberg, *Painting in July*, 360.

# 4

## THE SALA DELL' ALBERGO

Fig. 20. Jacopo Robusti called Tintoretto. *The Crucifixion* (1565) with gratitude for the generosity of the *Scuola Grande di San Rocco*.

The figure of Christ on the cross is presented iconically to viewers of the painting. If we imagine the positioning in plan form, the crucified image is thrust forward on the apex of a triangle. The only people within the painting who are able to view it are members of the mourning group huddled beneath it. And only three of them are actually viewing the crucified Christ: John the evangelist, Mary Magdalene, and an anonymous female figure who stands at the foot of the cross. They see what we the viewers also see: Christ in Majesty. It is a spiritual vision of what is there physically which is a mangled body. The mourning group are presented to us as a part of that vision and in that sense the central element of the painting represents eternity placed in the midst of violently passing time. We don't know what part of the vision is available to the viewers within the painting or to the viewers of the painting and it seems to me that this is the point Tintoretto makes. He asks, "What do you see: the brutal physicality of the Crucifixion that I represent by showing the cruelty inflicted upon the two thieves, or the spiritual reality available to those in a state of grace?"

I think that it is useful to remind ourselves of the original response to the claim that a crucified figure is the Savior of Mankind. Crucifixion was a common punishment at the time of Jesus. This is demonstrated in the reported disputation between the two thieves crucified with Jesus. It records that they were, unlike Jesus, being crucified, ". . .justly; for we receive the due reward of our deeds: but this man hath done nothing amiss."[1]

> Divinity . . . was for the very greatest of the great: for victors, and heroes, and kings. Its measure was the power to torture one's enemies not to suffer it oneself. That a man who had himself been crucified might be hailed as a god could not help but be seen by people everywhere across the Roman world as scandalous, obscene, grotesque . . . Not merely blasphemy, it was madness.[2]

Tintoretto's painting has to be seen in situ for its full impact to be experienced. It is simply overwhelming. Ruskin was

1. Luke 23:41 (KJV).
2. Holland, *Dominion*, xviii.

reportedly rendered dumb when he first viewed the painting. I understand that this, of itself, was a unique phenomenon! The scale of the painting is enormous.[3] It is beautifully preserved and after the 2018 renovations recording the five hundred years since the death of Tintoretto it is now well-lit. It is to be seen in the relatively small room at the far left side of the upper room, one floor up in *the Scuola Grande di San Rocco, Campo dei Frari,* Venice. Please visit if at all possible. The narrative detail of the work is intense and varied. This can initially confuse the viewer as the variety of activity and time in which the activities take place is presented as a single image. However, the groups of active participants are cleverly separated for us by the painter and the presentation of them as one unit seems to convey the spiritual purpose of the painting. This purpose appears to be to separate the figure of Christ from the vicissitudes of time in the viewer's imagination. This is particularly evident in the way that Tintoretto presents three crucifixion narratives as if they are taking place simultaneously and yet the narrative references indicate otherwise. The thief to the stage-left (in Latin the *sinister* side) is morally defined by his position. He has his back to Christ and is suffering the brutality of the process of crucifixion. He it is whom Luke tells us "railed on" Jesus for not exercising the power he is reported to possess to save himself and the two thieves. Therefore, in narrative terms, this exchange has yet to take place or, as related to the depiction of Jesus already crucified, it has previously taken place. The stage-right thief is being raised up with his eyes in contact with those of Christ. It is he whom Luke tells asks Jesus to remember him and in return receives Christ's promise of salvation. Again, according to which perspective we choose, it either has taken place or is yet to do so. And, of course, and perhaps primarily, although Christ is presented in an iconic *consummatum est* pose we are reminded by the two thief episodes of the violent brutality and cruel suffering of the sacrifice that has been undertaken willingly for us by the central figure presented as iconically timeless. There is a spiritual and physical three-dimensionality about the whole presentation.

3. 5.36 x 12.24 mtrs. or 17 x 40 ft.

Tintoretto's painting is profoundly and otherworldly spiritual but it gains impact by being also firmly and this worldly physical. The detail that Tintoretto devotes to background activity is quite extraordinary and it demands close attention. He spares no creative effort in firmly entrenching the fundamentally central event of his Christian faith in the passing world of here and now/ there and then in which you and I momentarily participate. In the upstage-right corner of the painting almost eclipsed by a beautifully drawn camel,[4] we glimpse the gates of Jerusalem. The camel is being led down the *via dolorosa* along which Christ has recently walked to his crucifixion. The two camel drivers chat about the day's events with one pointing along the path followed by Christ and many others during their lifetime in Jerusalem. In the further distance there passes a female camel rider little interested in what is a regular occurrence in the region. In front of these distant camel drivers, on a hill, there are, judging from their garments, groups of Jewish and Turkish inhabitants. There is also a group of mothers, one with a child to whom she speaks. Perhaps they had wept as Jesus passed and were told not to weep for him but for themselves and their children.[5] We are being asked to recognize something that at this time distance we may easily overlook: these were pre-Christian times. What we are being shown is the cosmic event that Christians believe transformed the world in which we live for ever. There are gentiles, Jews, and Ottomans surrounding the stage-like structure upon which the world-changing event is taking place. In the opposite, upper stage-left corner there are people passing on their way across a bridge. The bridge is being approached by two Orientals one of whom appears to be crippled and using a crutch. They show no interest in the events taking place in the distance from them. Way up in the sky to the stage-left of Christ's outstretched left arm there is what appears to be an eclipsed sun

4. The ideas that Tintoretto wishes to convey take precedent over painting technicalities such as perspective. Cf. Wilfred Owen writing on his first-world-war poetry, "Above all, I am not concerned with poetry . . . the poetry is in the pity."

5. Luke 23:8.

to remind us that "there was darkness over all the earth"[6] and to invite viewers/participators, as in all drama, to suspend disbelief.

With the ordinariness of the context thus established, we are plunged into the midst of the violent physical activity of the Crucifixion. The downstage right figure in front of the white horse captures this physicality in an almost tangible fashion. As he strains on the rope that is hoisting the 'good' thief's cross upright, he is one hundred per cent physical. He is, in fact, engaged in the most brutal, inhumane physical act that it is possible to imagine. He is also engaged in the most cosmically damning spiritual disaster that human kind has ever undertaken: the crucifixion of the Son of God. And yet the painter directs no blame upon him whatsoever. He is one of us earning his daily bread by being totally and mindlessly involved in hard physical work. The nature of this physical work is emphasized by Tintoretto's depiction of the mechanical details of the work. We are confronted with ladders, wedges, ropes and spades but mainly with human physical effort. Men are putting their backs into this work; they are not, as Christ observes on their behalf, exercised by knowing what they do.[7] They are presented as everyday laboring Venetians still to be seen working along the canals today. The disengaged, finely-dressed figures on horseback are not of that group. Such men, as Tintoretto well knew, were more likely to be uttering charitable sentiments in the *Sala dell' Albergo* than laboring along the canals. Tintoretto offers such the opportunity to refocus their lives as they survey the "wondrous cross" before undertaking their charitable mission. The man on horseback with the fine beard who is positioned center stage-left behind the man vigorously digging the vast hole into which the stem of the cross of the stage-left thief is to be placed demands attention. He places his left hand so complacently on his hip as he looks up at a job well-done: the end of a mouthy trouble-maker. No doubt, Tintoretto had a particular player in the drama in mind, perhaps Caiphas, the high priest who passed Jesus on to Pilate as the Jews under the colonial administration had no authority to

6. Luke 23:44–46 (KJV).
7. Luke 23:34 (KJV).

pass a sentence of crucifixion. His swagger and his fine clothing support such a suggestion. To his stage-left there is a Turkish figure also finely mounted and of official standing. The seedy mundanity of it all is conveyed in this corner of the painting as the soldiers in front of the digging man cower in the shadows gambling over the cloth of the crucified Christ's garments. On the opposite side, center stage-right and seated on a beautiful white horse there is a far more sympathetic character. He appears to be a condottiere[8] and the pose of his magnificent horse immediately recalls that of the bronze horses above the central porch of St. Mark's Basilica. He points to the crucified Christ and the purport of his words may be read in the face of the servant whom he addresses. Clearly, this figure is representative of Venetian piety.

The mourning group downstage-center of the painting is, along with the crucified Christ, the main component of the work, of course. It is at one with the Cross itself as a unified and timeless vision. The group in fact conceals the basis of the cross as being firmly implanted in the ground. This adds emphasis to the sense of a timeless visionary experience as it appears to float above the earth. The group is comprised of the three Mary's (the Mother of Christ and her sister and the Magdalene) John the evangelist, Joseph of Arimathea, Nicodemus, and two other women. The Mother of Jesus is depicted with her arms spread in a crucified position implying that spiritually she has also been crucified. John is beatifically looking up at the glorified Christ. The contrast between the surrounding mundanity and the monumentally idealized mourning group, appearing as at one with the cross make a powerful spiritual impact. Rising above the backs of the mourners there is a woman with arms and hands spread as she looks upwards. She forms a link uniting the group with the upward stem of the Cross of Christ in an attitude of adoration.[9] They are the permanent timeless feature around which all the rest is momentarily passing.

Apart from the anonymity of the background figures, the workers and the soldiers, and the stage-left and stage-right

8. See note 28 *The Scuola Grande*.
9. Which, very succinctly imagined, is the role of Mother Church.

horse-backed figures of authority there are a number of stand-out faces that appear to be profoundly involved and may well be meant to portray members of the brotherhood personally responding to the awesome event and with whom we might wish to align ourselves: they had their moment; as we view/participate in the painting that moment is now ours. The first of these is very precisely and effectively placed. I referred to the condottiere figure center stage-right as representative of Venetian piety. He is a magnificent figure in full armor and he appears to be teaching his young servant proper respect. The military man's magnificent helmet and sword lie on the ground in front of him next to a memorial tablet recording the name of Tintoretto's patron, the *Guardian Grande* of the *Scuola* at the time: Girolamo Rota. In the context of the painting these may be viewed as very human attempts to attach permanence to passing time, tucked away in the corner of the painting as the armor of famous warriors gets tucked away in the corners of museums. The magnificent white horse with its allusion to Saint Mark's Basilica is depicted by Tintoretto's positioning as a two-headed creature. Curving away to its left is the head and front body of a humble, dull-colored donkey. Mounted on this donkey with his head appearing from behind the head of the white horse is the head of a white, gaunt figure completely "lost" in the awesomeness of what he is witnessing. Tintoretto makes a very powerful visual endorsement of the Council of Trent's demands for each individual to take personal responsibility for the integrity of their spiritual life. Official piety may be very decorative but personal spirituality is hidden away from human eyes and far more important and demanding. The burden of responsibility borne by the old to inculcate this understanding in the young is, of course, fundamental to the Christian gospel.[10] Tintoretto presents an example of undertaking the responsibility of nurturing the young that differs from that of the condottiere figure. The older man in question wears a blue robe, he has white beard, and he is situated

---

10. Luke 17:2 (KJV). It were better for him that a mill-stone were hanged about his neck and he cast into the sea, than he should offend one of these little ones.

center stage-right just below the mother and baby. To his left there is a young man of similar age to the servant of the condottiere. The white horse is replaced by a donkey. The old man does not point and speak. He gazes with his palm spread in wonder setting an example. Two approaches, then, dictated by the different roles in which the teachers are cast. However, perhaps Tintoretto suggests that humility, a prerequisite of the *Scuola's* approach is more easily arrived at on a donkey than it is on a condottiere's white stallion. If we move to the stage-left, leaning on the raised platform there is a bald figure looking up at the cross with folded arms clearly puzzled and, in contrast to the older man immediately behind him, undecided. On his stage-right side leaning on the wall of the platform is a man more finely dressed with a similar intently puzzled gaze at proceedings. Whereas the bald man may well be a member of the brotherhood, the well-dressed man's clothing suggests he is Jewish as, of course, is Christ. One can imagine the confusion in the mind of the Jewish onlooker. Both are challenged in different ways. Tintoretto populates the crowd not only with people from different religious and national backgrounds but also from different periods. Some are contemporary with the historical period of the events, others with the contemporary period of the painting. We can even choose to make them as timeless as the ideas they illustrate or to adopt them into our own period. The painting demands the participation of the viewer to complete it.

Finally, although the event took place before the death of Christ, of course, clinging to the ladder, the man with the sponge on a hyssop stem is dipping it in vinegar with which to torment Christ. The man behind on the black mule leans complacently forward. His job is done. He's bored. His important function was to strip the leaves off the hyssop stem. In a wonderfully poignant touch, the mule is being allowed to eat the leaves before they retire.

# CONCLUDING REMARKS

*C*aritas is the Latin word that translates as Charity which is rather unfortunate as the English word "charity" has become encrusted with connotations that detract from the purity of the Latin word. This is clearly demonstrated by the idioms that involve the word "charity": *charity begins at home; as cold as charity,* for example. The word is associated with the giving of money often resentfully and for public demonstration of one's praiseworthy beneficence. I find the word "caring" much more appropriate for that with which *the Scuola Grande di San Rocco* was intended to be concerned. It is caring, I suggest, that Tintoretto's paintings are fundamentally about. It is increasingly clear to me that "caring" is the most important human quality to be cultivated and to cherish. It is the powerful sense of the caring attitude to his subject matter and the characters involved that, for me, makes Tintoretto the great artist that he undoubtedly is. "The characters involved" include, of course, us the viewers of the paintings. Vasari[1] wrote, after visiting Venice and viewing Tintoretto's work, including *The Crucifixion* in the *Sala dell' Albergo,* that Tintoretto was "the most extraordinary brain that the art of painting has produced." Art historians seem to have been, and maybe still are, a little reluctant to become too emotionally involved in their responses. Vasari had strong intellectual objections to the style of Tintoretto's paintings

---

1. Georgio Vasari (1511–1574) was an Italian painter, architect, writer, and historian, best known for his *Lives of the Most Excellent Painters, Sculptors, and Architects.*

but all credit to him for not allowing that to prevent him from admitting that there was a power in the paintings that he found it hard to articulate: "a lot of brain" doesn't quite hack it. Almost exactly 400 years later, in 1962, a person with whom I correspond had just graduated and had a job as a tour guide that involved a trip to the *Scuola Grande di San Rocco*. He found that he was unable to evoke much interest in the paintings or to prompt any verbal response from his group. However one brave soul did his best: "That Tintoretto seems to have used an awful lot of paint."

I imply that charity can often be no indication of *caritas* and, of course, caring can also be a rather vacuous performance. In a determination not to be seen as cynical, we may be easily deceived. As Ruskin[2] pointed out in one of his essays in *Unto This Last*, a bad person doesn't become a good person simply by espousing a new set of ideas: a radical change is required within that person: the person has to be, as it were, born again. In this sense, *caritas* is a spiritual condition and an individual responsibility as King Lear realizes in the quotation on the epigram page at the beginning of this book. Tintoretto clearly understands and promotes this perception through his view of humanity and its destiny offered by the Christian faith. throughout the cycle of paintings in the *Scuola*.[3] He does this by challenging the façades behind which we take refuge. In the *Sala Terrena* he removes the sentimentality that often clouds our thinking when imaging events such as *The Annunciation* or *The Adoration of the Magi*. *The Massacre of the Innocents* is almost impossible to look into closely so vividly does it ask us to look at our human nature.[4] The association in *The Adoration of the Magi* between the Virgin with her offering of the Son of God and the poor woman with her offering of two doves is beyond thought-provoking. In the two final paintings either side of the

---

2. John Ruskin (8 February 1819 to 20 January 1900) was the leading English art critic of the Victorian age.

3. Obviously, this does not mean that one has to be a Christian to be moved by the paintings of Tintoretto: King Lear was not a Christian, but then again, he had not viewed Tintoretto's paintings.

4. However, if we do look closely, we are given the consolation of image 8.

altar of *Female Saints Reading in a Landscape* Tintoretto invites us to take time to quietly withdraw from the riot of life to put our own individual lives in order.

Moving up to *The Sala Superiore* we are further immersed in the spirituality of *caritas* with *The Adoration of the Shepherds*. In the hayloft we have the Virgin presenting God's gift to the world– the supreme act of *CARITAS* captured in John's Gospel.

> For God so loved the world, that he gave his only begot-
> ten Son,[5]

She presents that gift to the poor, bare-breasted symbol of human *caritas* opposite thus sanctifying it as a condition worthy of our devotion. *The Last Supper* gives us another association of divinity with poverty similar to that in *The Adoration of the Magi* downstairs. This time, the head of the half-naked beggar in front of us eyeing his gift of bread is lined up with head of Christ at the far perspective point offering the Eucharist wafer to Peter. Here, poverty is aligned with the supreme act of *CARITAS* as Christ offers his broken body to his disciples that Christians believe they receive at the Eucharist. And so the message is delivered time and again by the inspired hand of Tintoretto. On the opposite wall, *The Miracle of the Loaves and Fishes* with all the needy human beings in the foreground caring for one another recalls the brotherhood to their sacred obligations. In the brightly-lit background the breast-feeding symbols of charity unite the two English translations of the original word—caring and charity— for the dominant theme of Tintoretto's work: *CARITAS*.

---

5. John 4:16 (KJV).

Fig. 21 Jacopo Robusti called Tintoretto. *The Crucifixion* (detail). PD
Wikimedia Commons.

Finally, to *The Sala dell'Albergo* and the overwhelming *Crucifixion*. As mentioned earlier, Ruskin was struck dumb by the painting and I think that this is probably not a bad way to respond. But I must just mention in closing what I find the most moving and sympathetic response to the event within the painting itself: the beautiful simplicity of it underlies its profundity. It is the downstage right image of the apparently two-headed creature. The stage-right head is that of a magnificent white stallion; the stage-left head is that of a humble dull donkey. From behind the head of the white horse peers a bald white head of a worn old man who is in fact mounted on the donkey. He stares up aghast at the crucified son of God. He is struck dumb. And so am I.

# BIBLIOGRAPHY

Austin, Michael. *Explorations In Art, Theology and Imagination*. London: Equinox, 2005.

Dixon, John W. *Art and the Theological Imagination*. New York: Seabury, 1978.

———. "Painting as Theological Thought: The Issues in Tuscan Theology." http://www.unc.edu/-jwdixon/articles/tuscan.html

Freedberg, S. J. *Painting in Italy 1500–1600*. Harmondsworth, UK: Penguin, 1971.

Grabski, Józef. "The Group of Paintings by Tintoretto in the "Sala Terrena" in the Scuola Di San Rocco in Venice and Their Relationship to the Architectural Structure." *Artibus Et Historiae* 1, no. 1 (1980): 115–31. Accessed June 5, 2020. doi:10.2307/1483132.

Holland, Tom. *Dominion, The Making of the Western Mind*. London: Little, Brown, 2019.

Manno, Antonio. *Tintoretto The Crucifixion in the Scuola Grande di San Rocco in Venice*. Venice: Marsilio Editori, 2013.

Miravalle, Mark. *With Jesus: the Story of Mary Co-redemtrix*. Goleta: Queenship, 1993.

Nichols, Tom. "Tintoretto, *prestezza* and the *poligrafi*: a study in the literary and visual culture of Cinquecento Venice." *Renaissance Studies* 10 no 1, 71–99.

———. *Tintoretto, Tradition and Identity*. London: Reaktion, 1999.

Paul, Benjamin. "Jacopo Tintoretto and the Church of San Benedetto in Venice." *Mitteilungen des Kunsthistorischen Institutes in Florenz* 49. Bd., H. 3 (2005) 388 and 402 note 64.

Sperling, Jutta Gisela. "Allegories of Charity and the Practice of Poor Relief at the Scuola Grande Di San Rocco." *Wallraf-Richartz-Jahrbuch* 70 (2009): 119–46. Accessed June 14, 2020. www.jstor.org/stable/24667668. 129

Viladesau, Richard. *The Beauty of the Cross: The Passion of Christ in Theology and the Arts from the Catacombs to the Eve of the Renaissance*. Oxford: Oxford University Press, 1999.

# INDEX

Lightning Source UK Ltd.
Milton Keynes UK
UKHW020841171220
375377UK00005B/68